Steve

MW01713008

DISCOVERING

WILDFLOWERS

A LITTLE AUSTRALIAN GIFT BOOK

www.steveparish.com.au

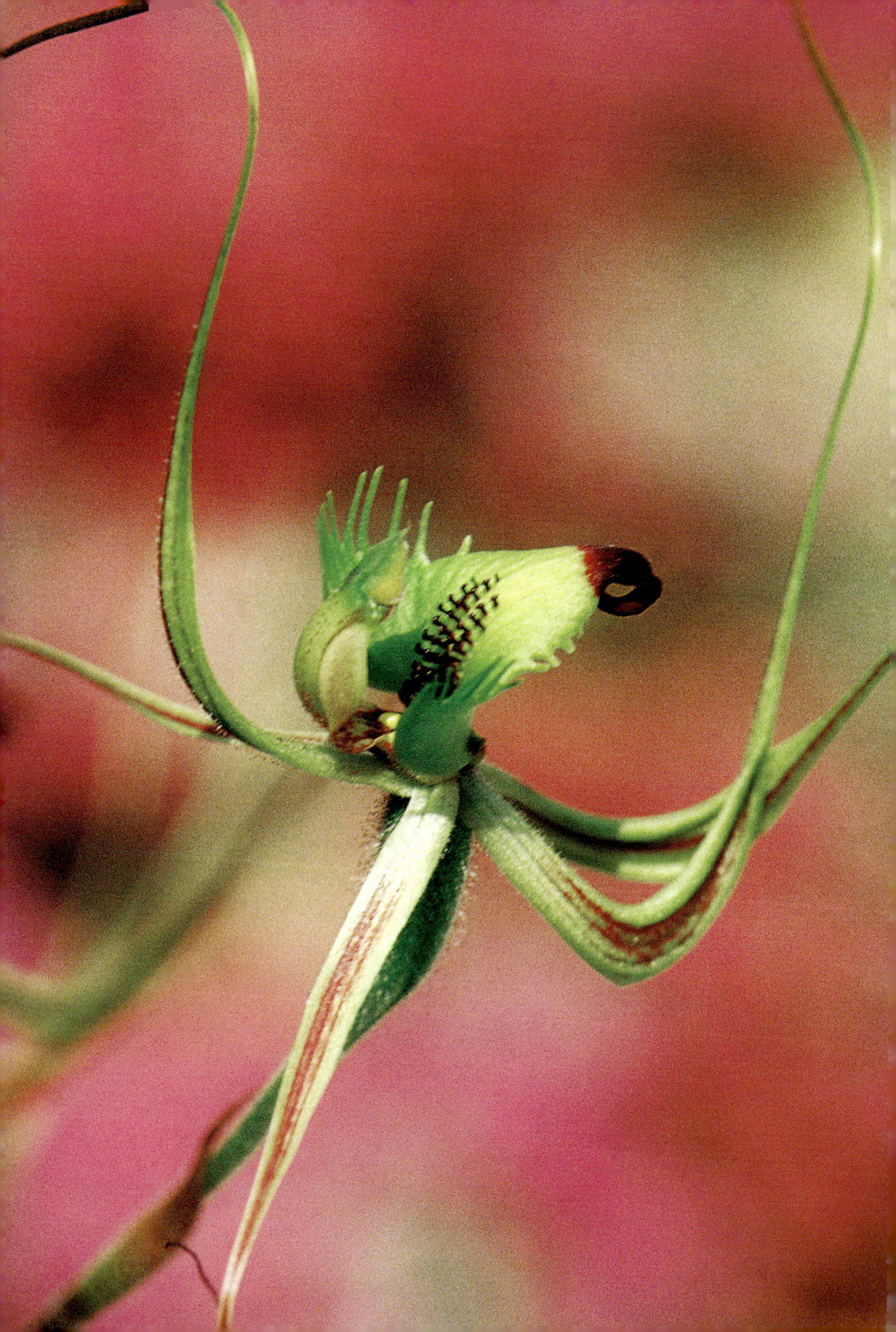

A GARDEN OF EDEN

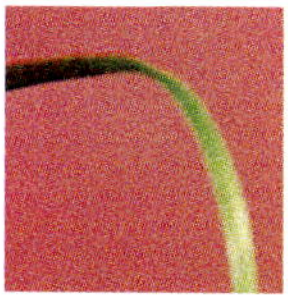

Earth, of all the known planets, is just the right distance from the sun to receive enough warmth for life to be sustained. Because of the warmth, water will stay liquid so it can dissolve the materials that plants and animals need for life.

Australia is an ancient land with a great variety of natural environments, all of which support plant life. Even in the harshness of the Red Centre, after life-giving rain falls, the desert blooms.

It was a diverse and unique flora that greeted 15th- and 16th-century naturalists on voyages of discovery to this unknown southern land. They returned to Europe with vast collections of Australia's flowering plants which bewildered and excited scientists.

The interests of science were of little concern to the early settlers. The Australian bush was just something to be cleared for agriculture or harvested for timber. Their love of plants remained tied to the familiar ornamentals of their homelands. Many of these plants migrated with the settlers.

Although many native species did not survive the nation-building process, Australians today appreciate the intrinsic value of this country's remarkable plant life.

Front cover: **Yellow-flowering eucalypt blossom.**

Page 2: **Fringed Mantis Orchid *Caladenia dilatata var. falcata.***

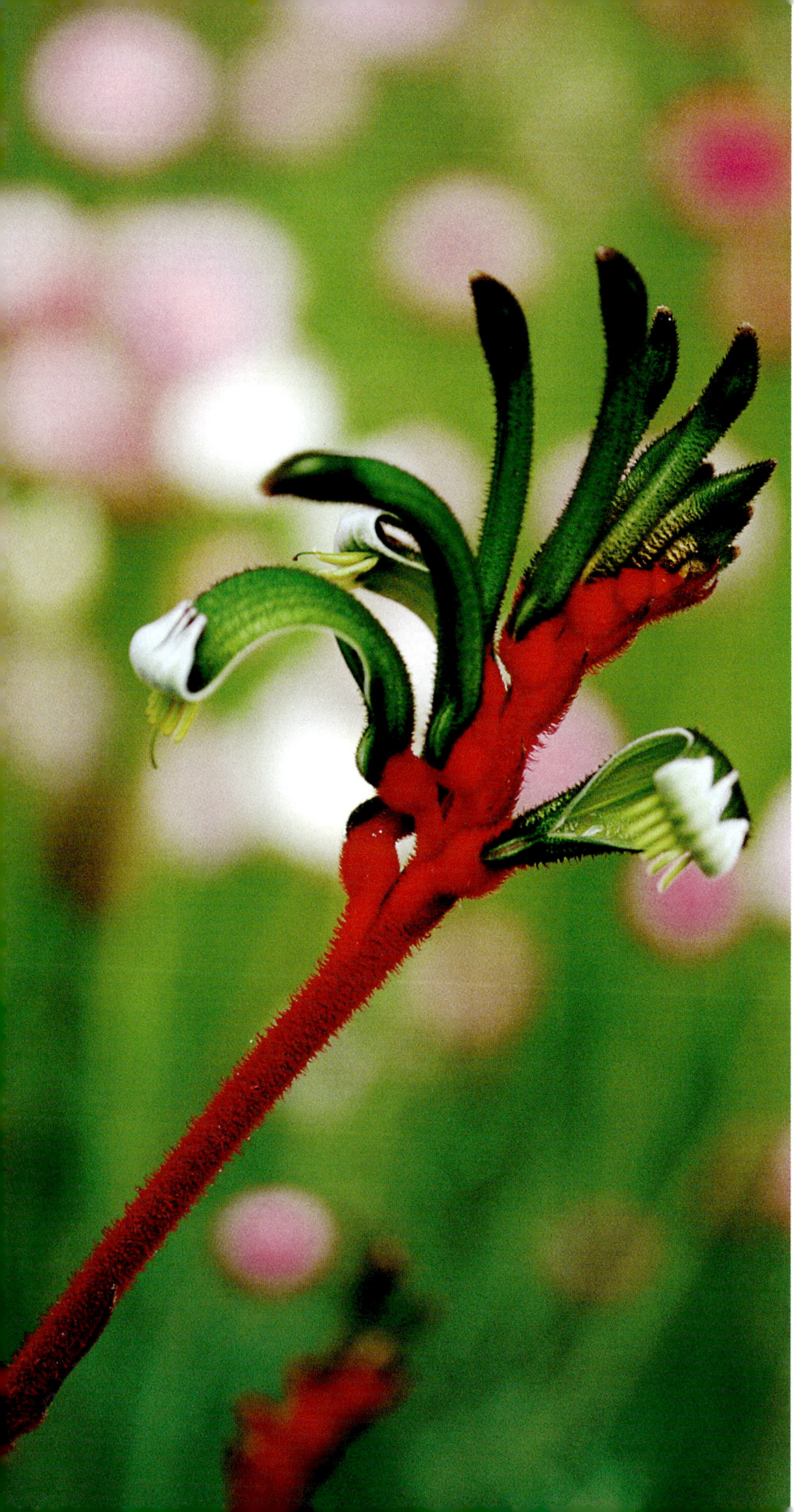

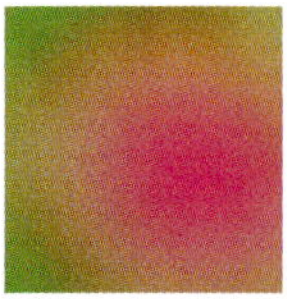

Left:

Mangles's Kangaroo Paw, *Anigozanthos manglesii.*

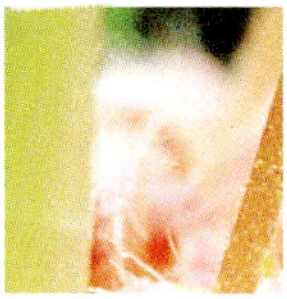

Right:

Mountain Devil, ***Lambertia formosa.***

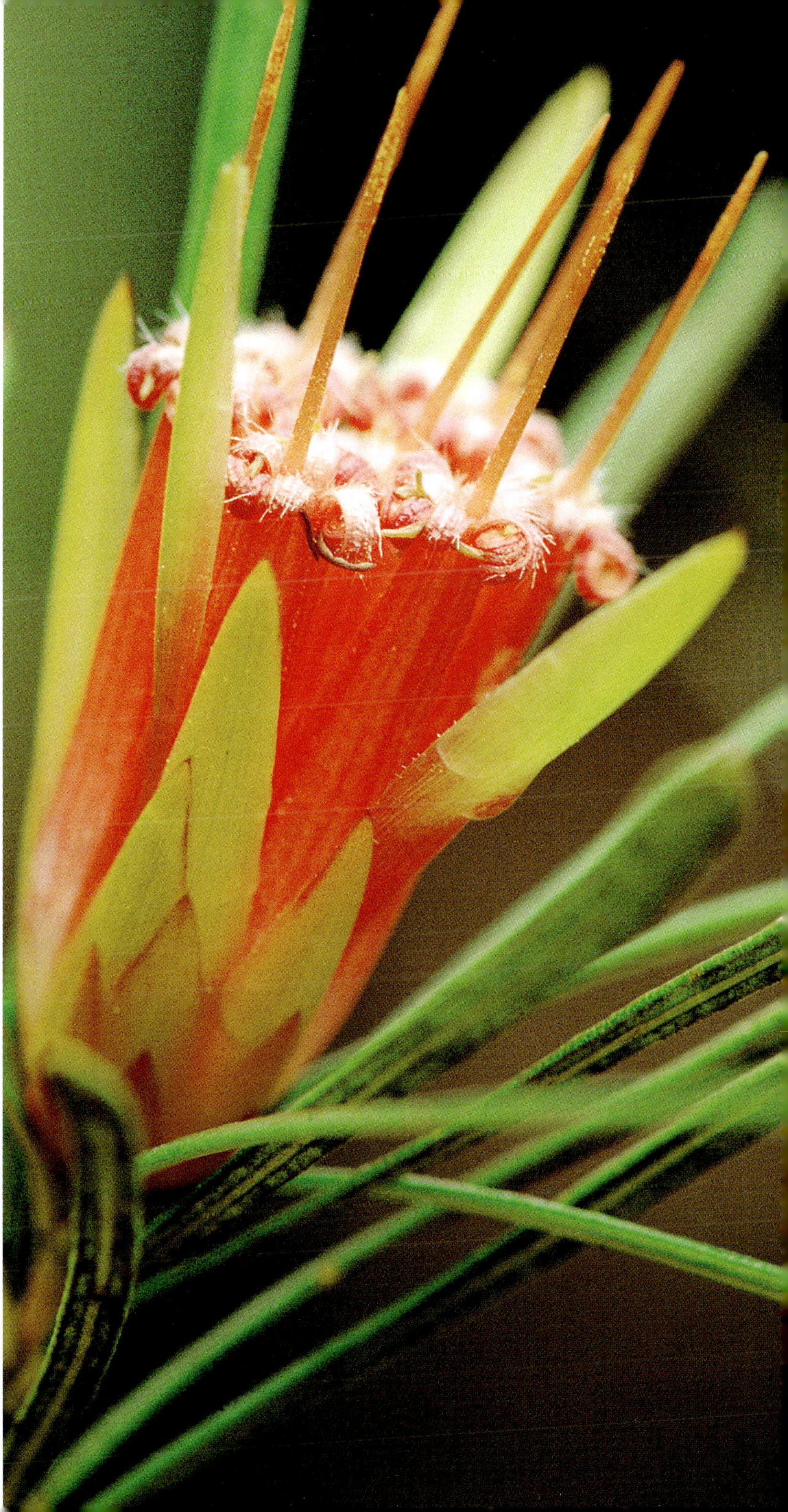

EXPERTS IN ADAPTABILITY

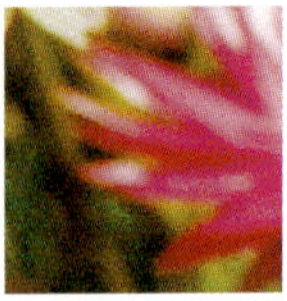

Armed with strategies developed in isolation over millions of years, flowering plants have exploited Australia's incredible range of environments. With a flourish of colour and form, plant communities cover a spectrum of habitats ranging from central arid sandplains to the northern wet tropics.

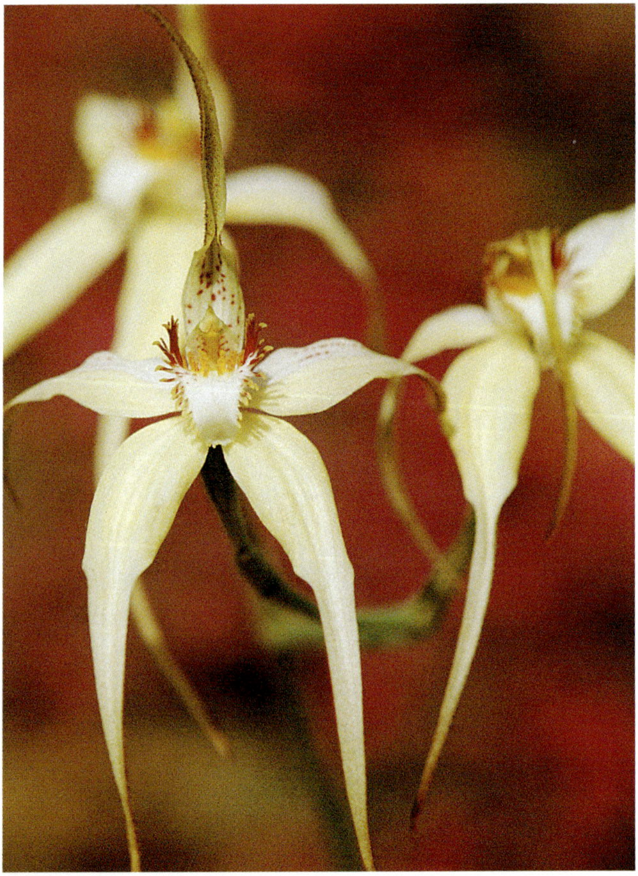

Right: **Common Spider Orchid, *Caladenia patersonii.***

Page 7: **Everlasting Daisies, *Helipterum roseum.***

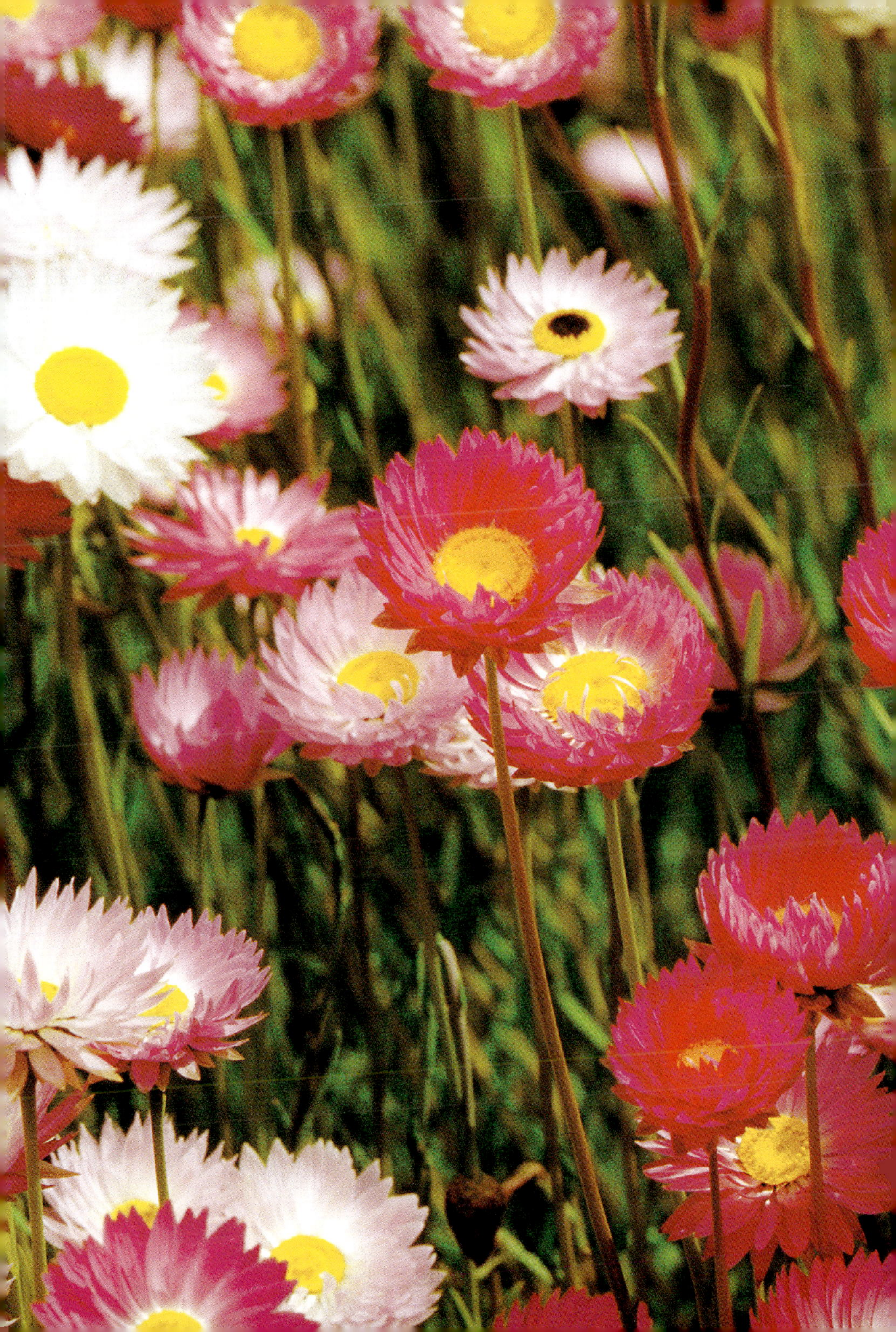

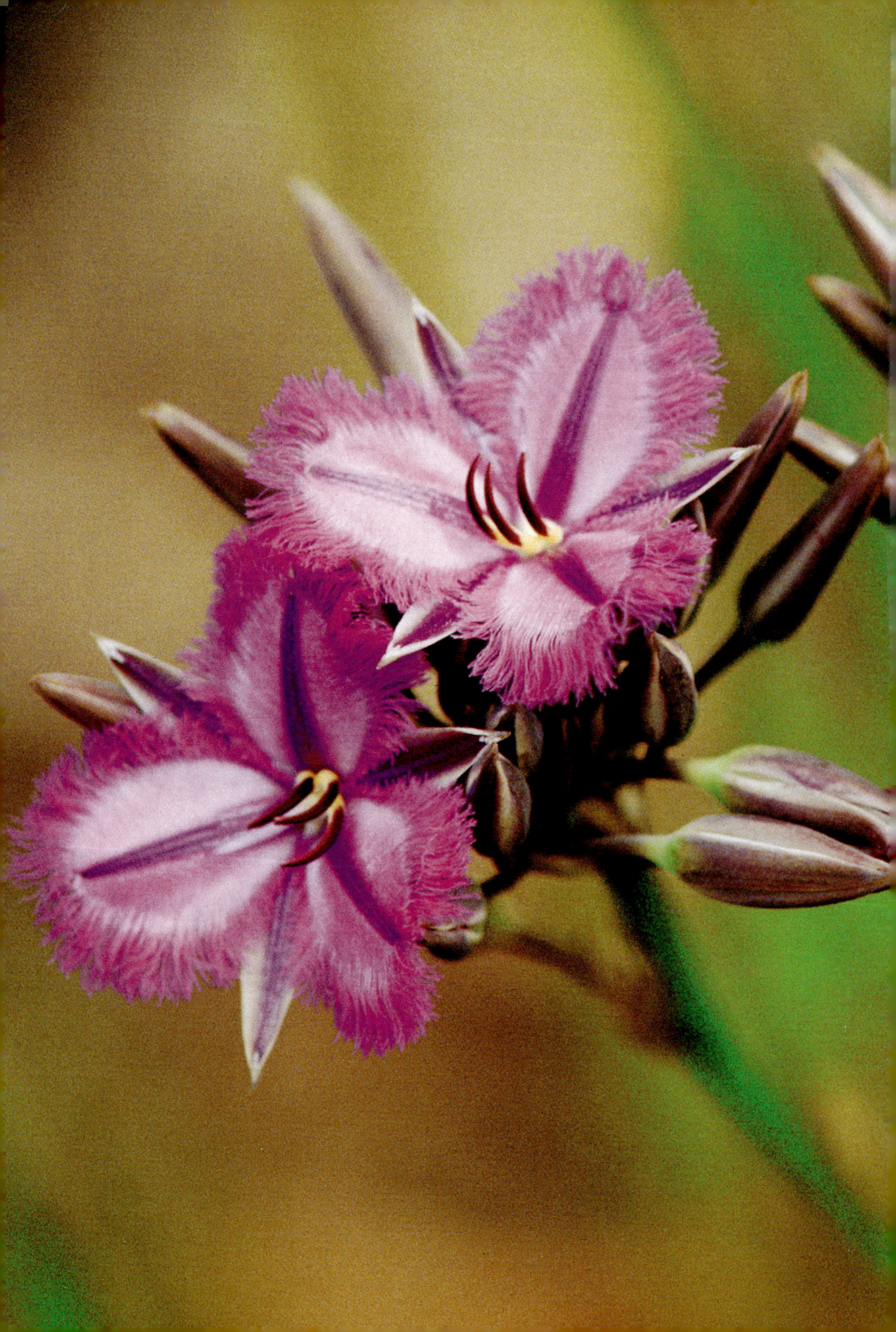

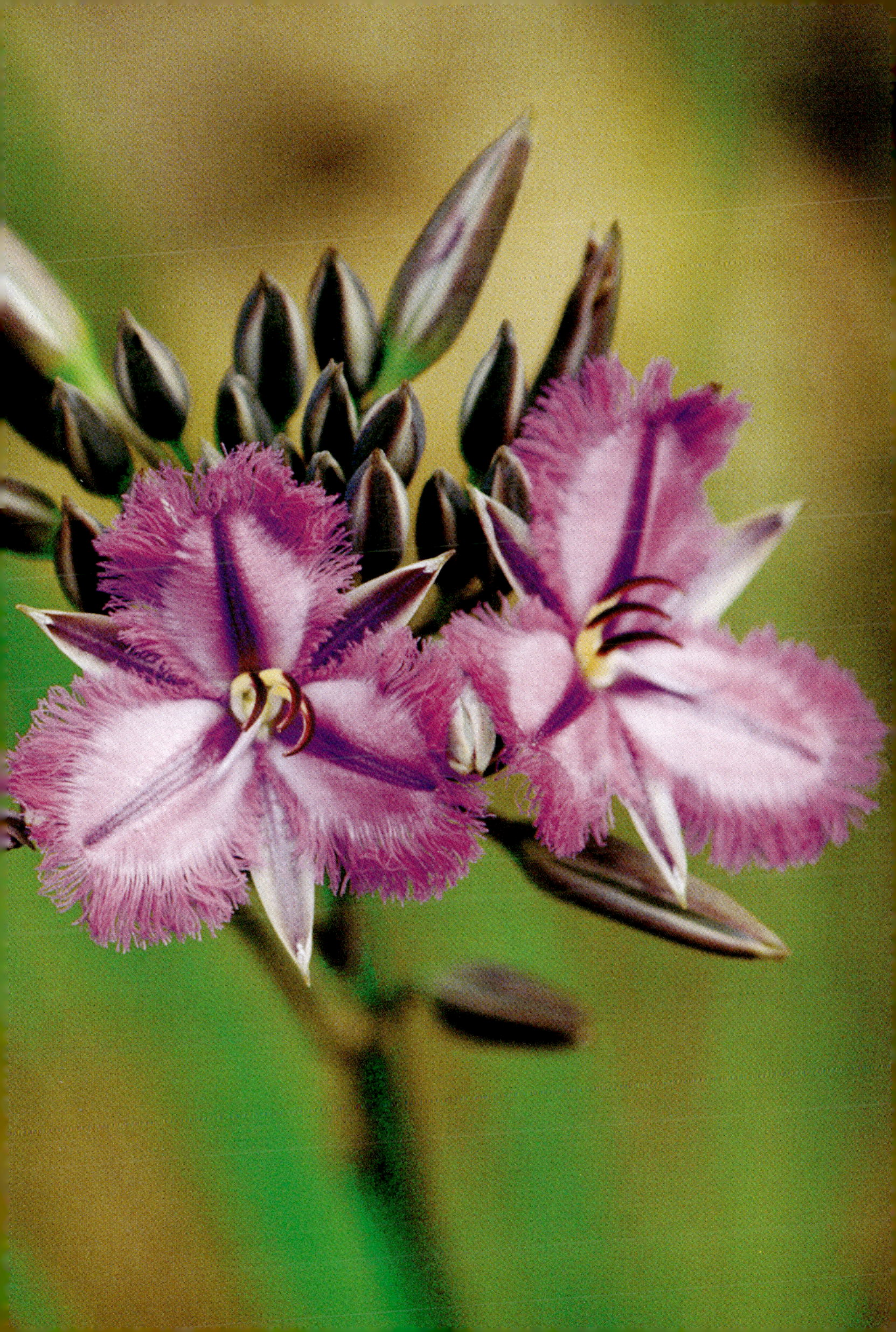

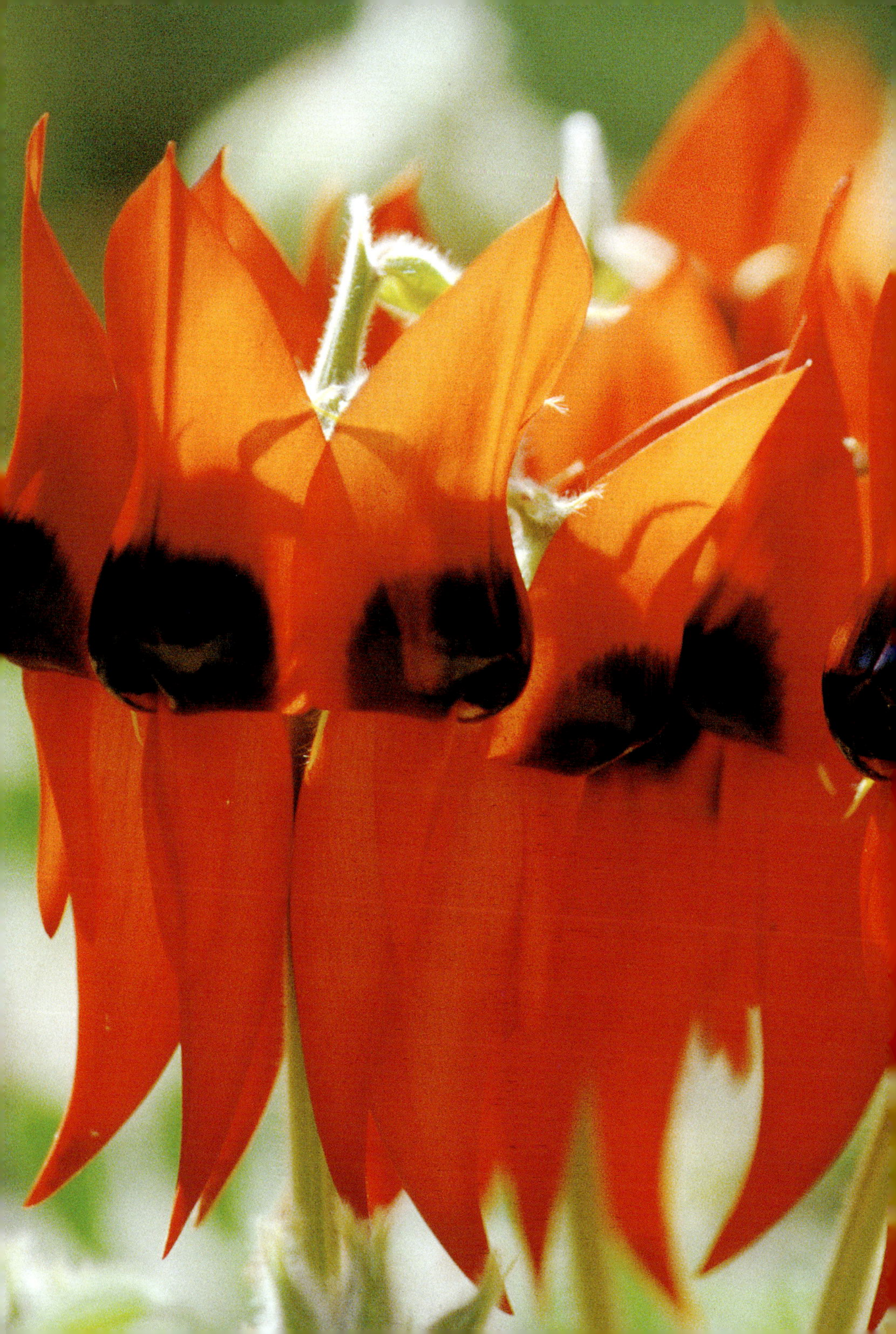

RENEWAL

Sporadic rain brings a riot of colour to shifting desert sands. Ephemeral flowers blossom and seed quickly, leaving dormant offspring to await the next fall of life-giving water.

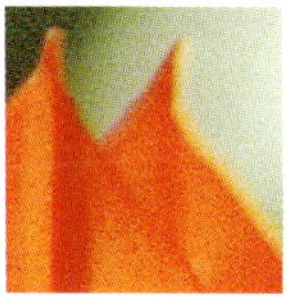

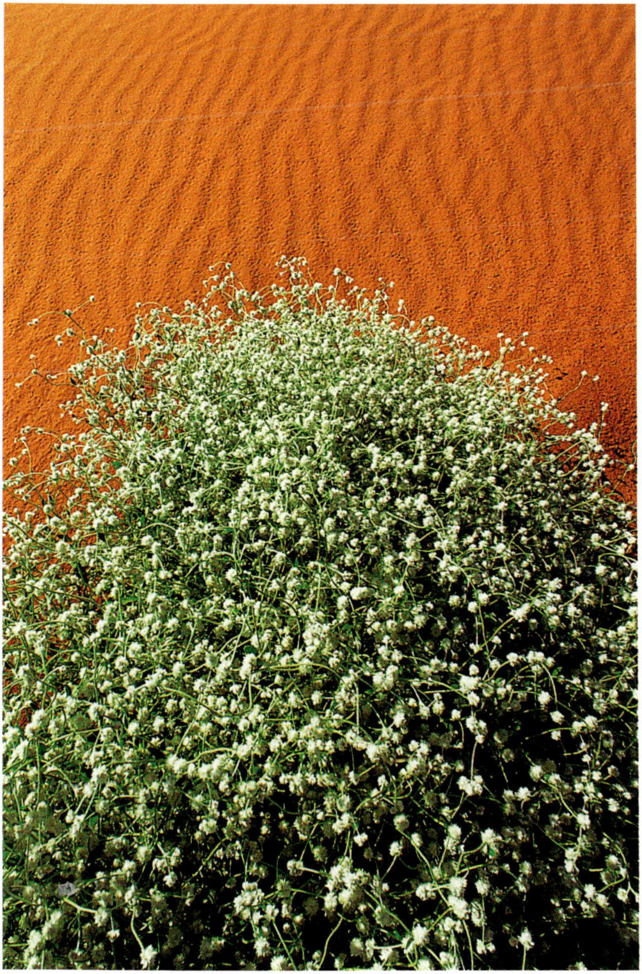

Pages 8–9:
The many-flowered Fringed Lily, *Thysanotus multiflorus.*

Page 10:
Sturt's Desert Pea, *Clianthus formosus.*

Left:
The desert shrub *Ptilotus sp.*

BANNERS OF WELCOME

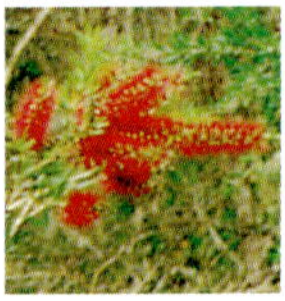

The profuse flowering of woodland trees and shrubs is a welcome herald of spring. The sweet promises of multi-hued blossoms entice small animals to become couriers of pollen.

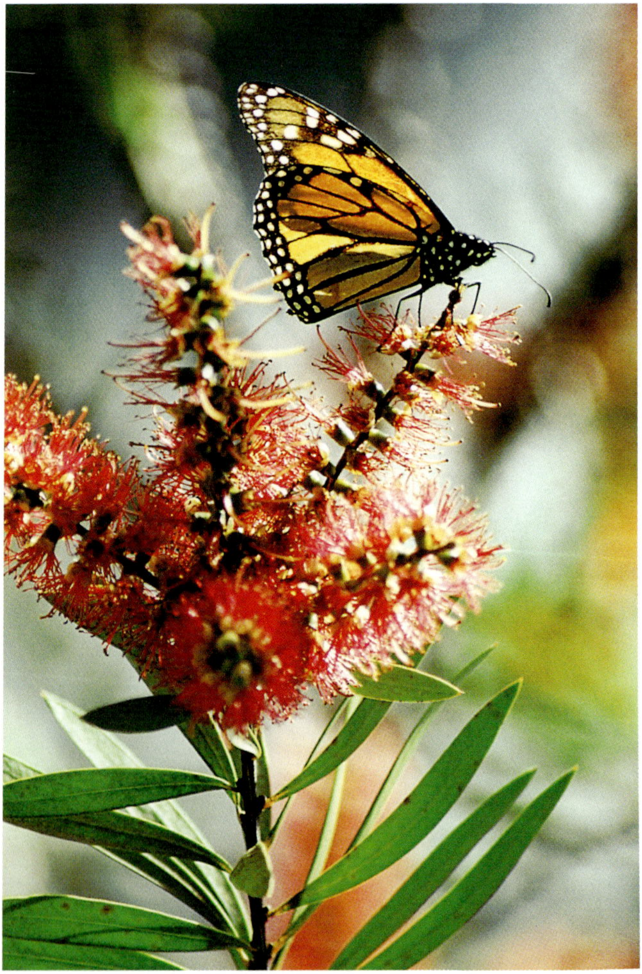

Right:
The Wanderer butterfly, on Gawler Hybrid, *Callistemon* "Harkness", is an insect pollinator.

Page 13:
Spring arrives in the woodland.

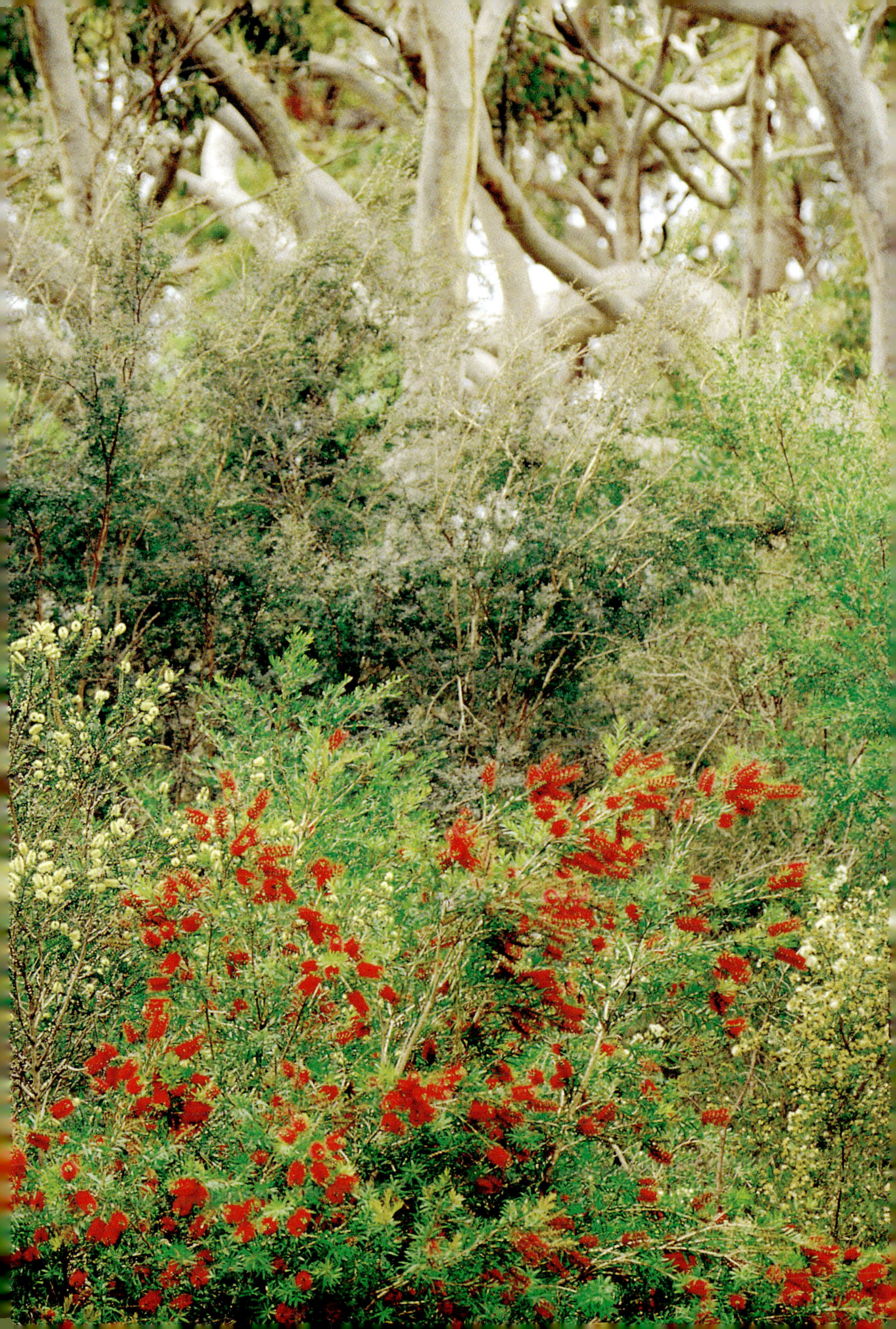

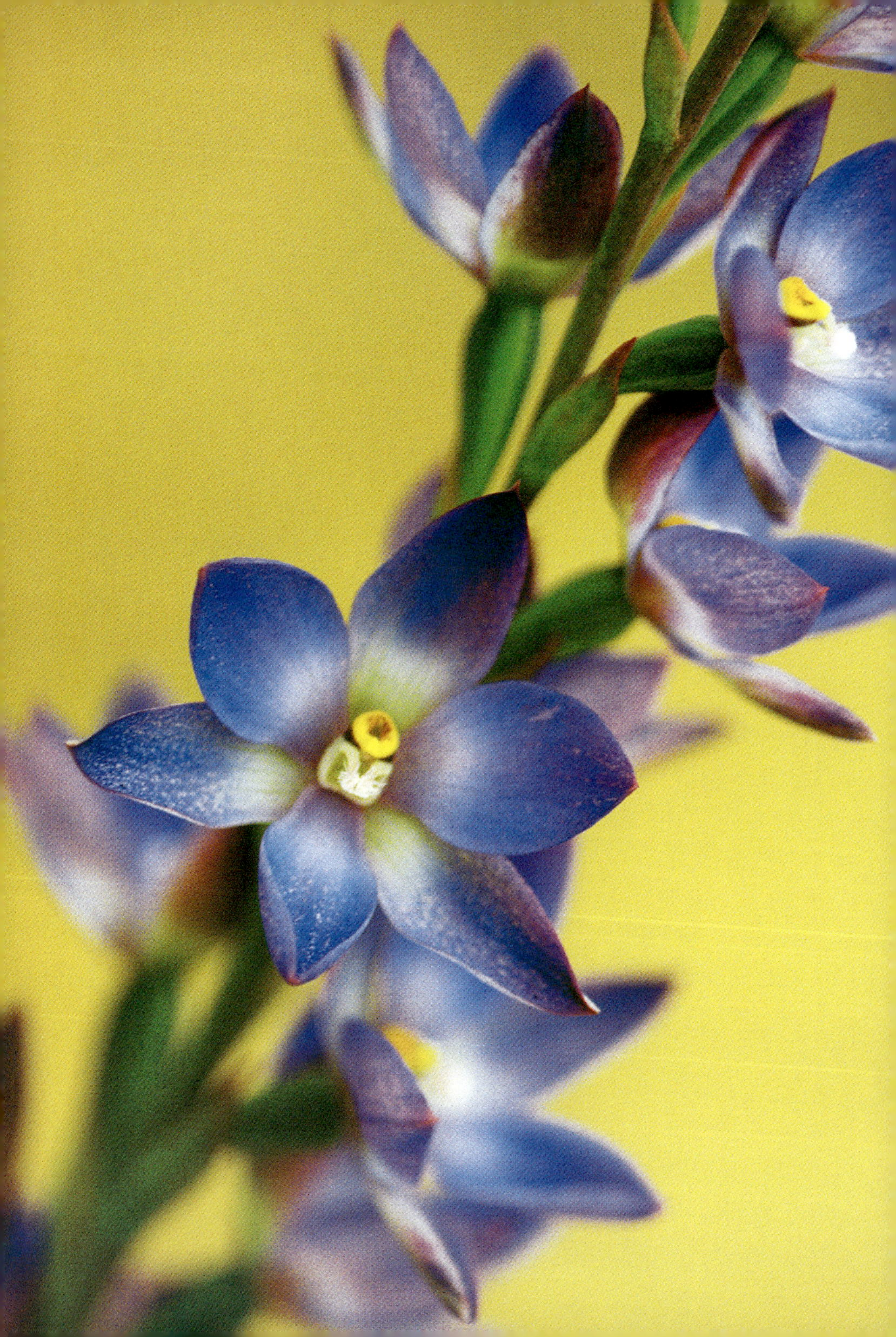

CHANGING SEASONS

Seasonal wildflowers paint the rainforests, woodlands, grassy plains, alpine meadows and coastal heaths with an ever-changing palette of colours. This stunning floral extravaganza peaks from mid-winter through spring.

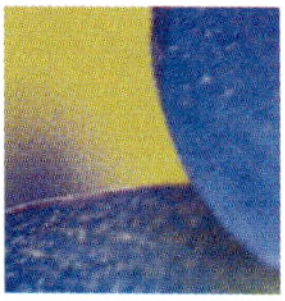

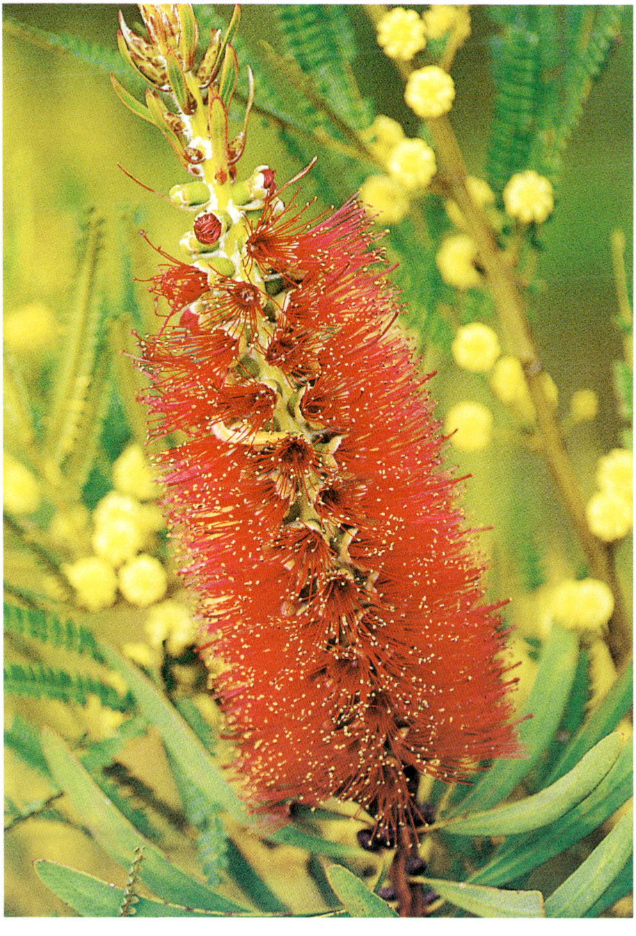

Page 14:
The scented Great Sun-orchid, *Thelymitra aristata.*

Left:
Red Bottlebrush, *Callistemon speciosus.*

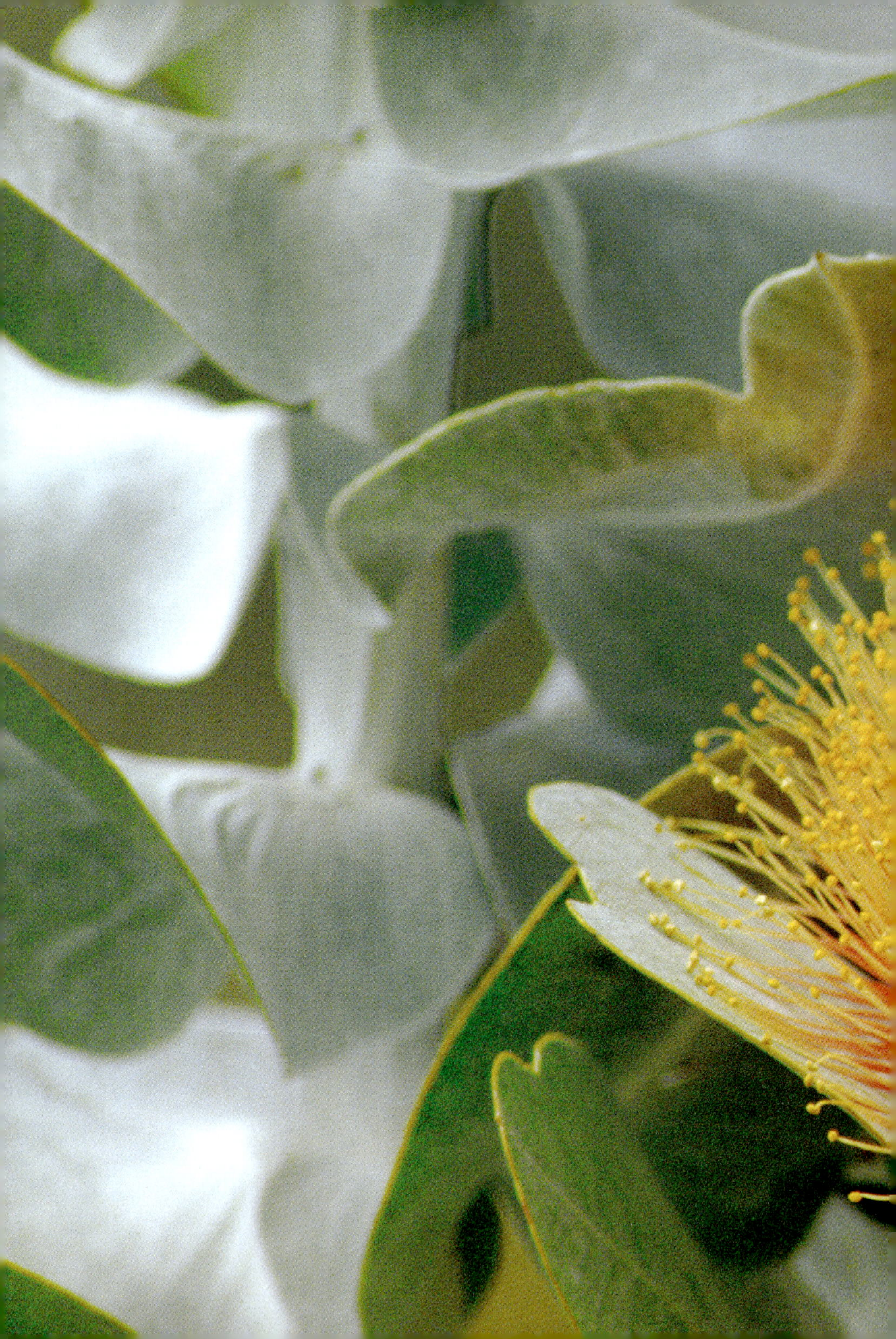

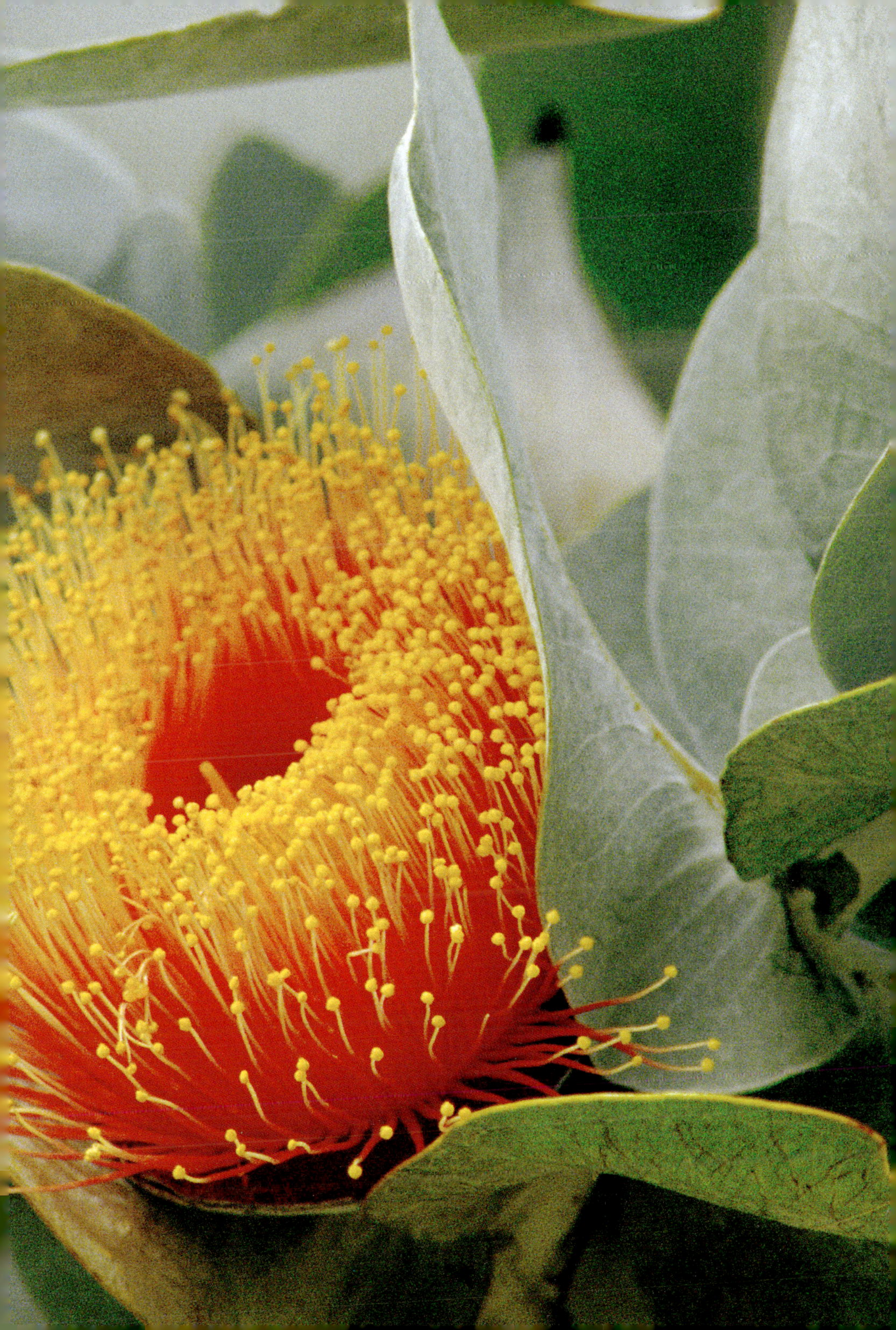

SURVIVAL

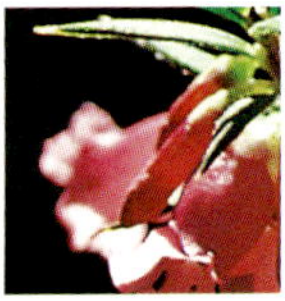

Dainty, softly-tinted flowers belie the tough nature of Australia's heathland plants. These compact, prickly survivors make the most of nutrient-poor soils and minimal rain. They can be found clinging to alpine meadows, dominating coastal plains or forming impenetrable barriers beneath woodland trees.

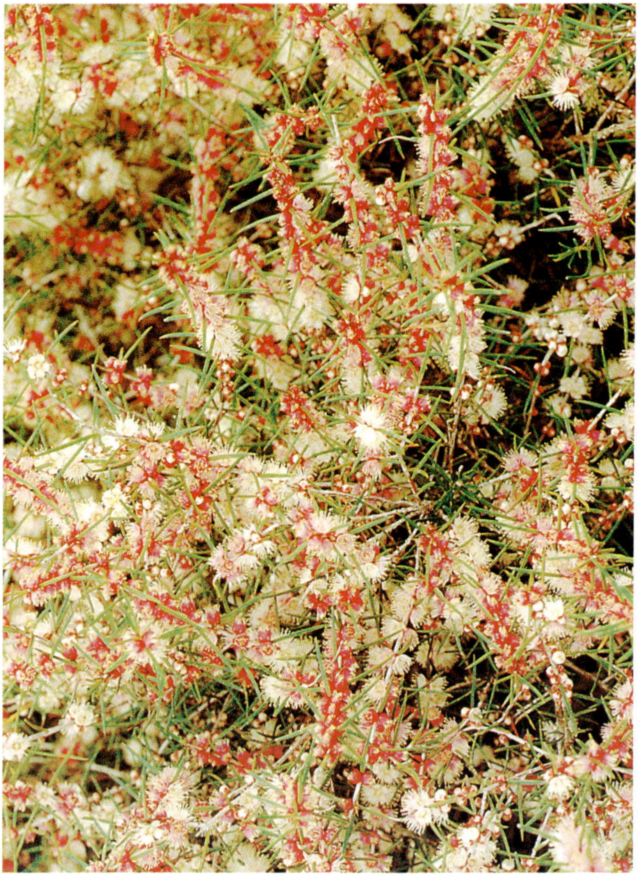

Pages 16–17: **Mottlecah, *Eucalyptus macrocarpa.***

Right: **White Myrtle, *Hypocalymma angustifolium.***

Page 19: **Victorian Heath, *Epacris impressa.***

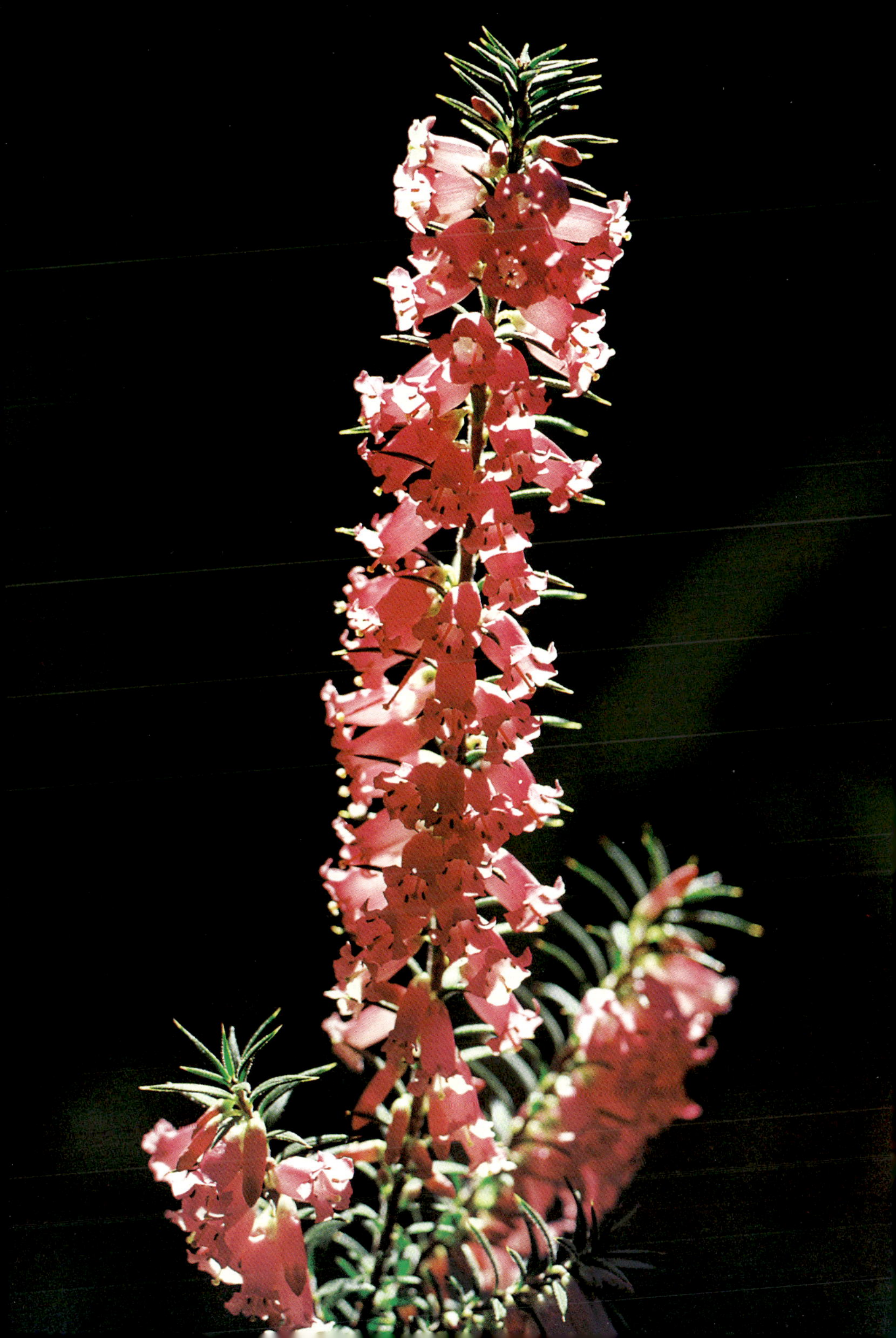

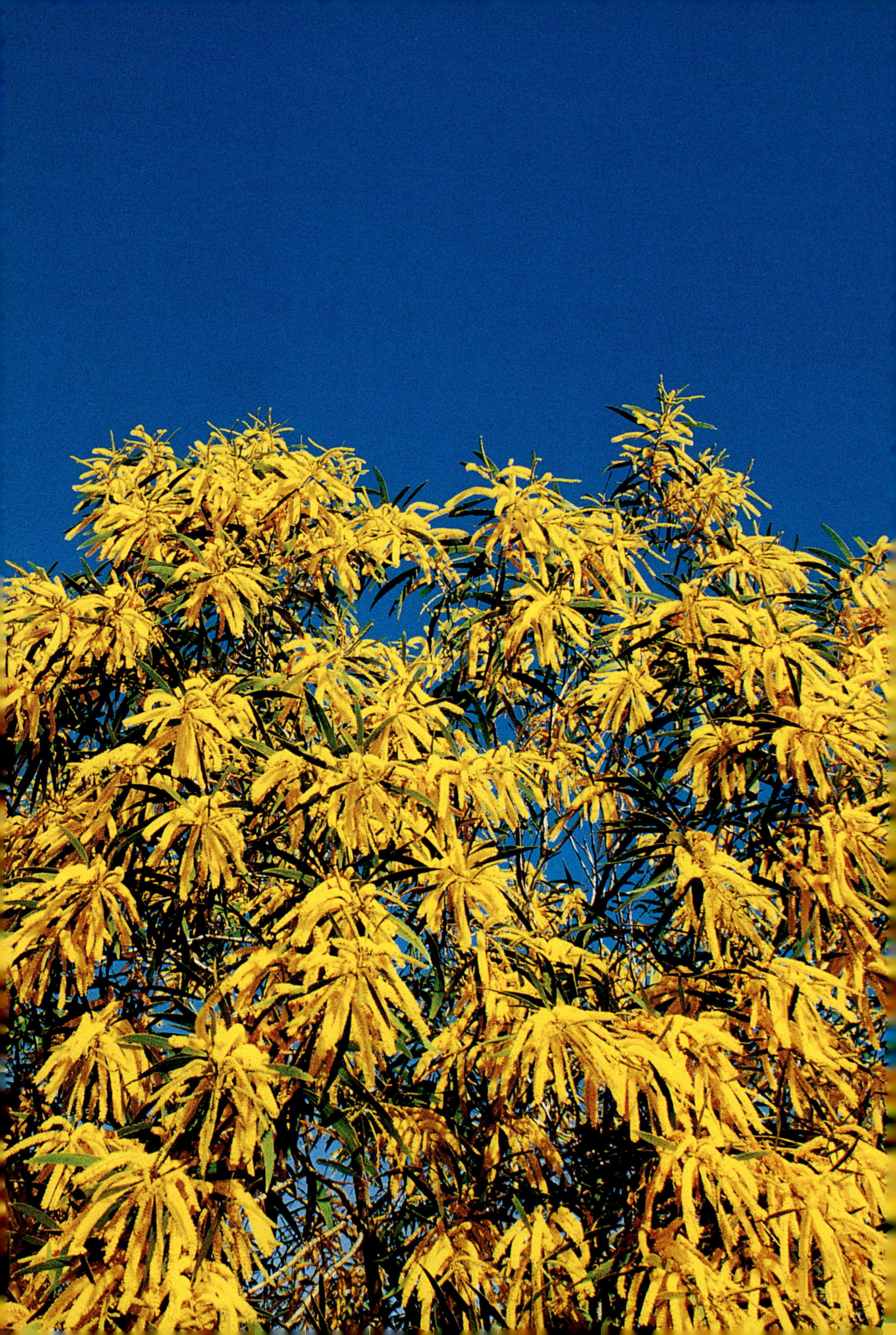

NATURE'S GIFT

Dormancy ends
as seeds give birth
in spring's warm light
and rain-softened earth.

A flash of pink,
A hint of blue
shadowed by leaves
and mirrored in dew.

Sunbursts of yellow,
pinwheels of flame
colour the way
in life's endless game.

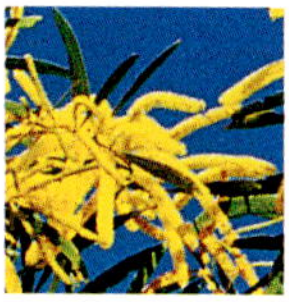

Page 20:
A shower of pale yellow wattle flowers.

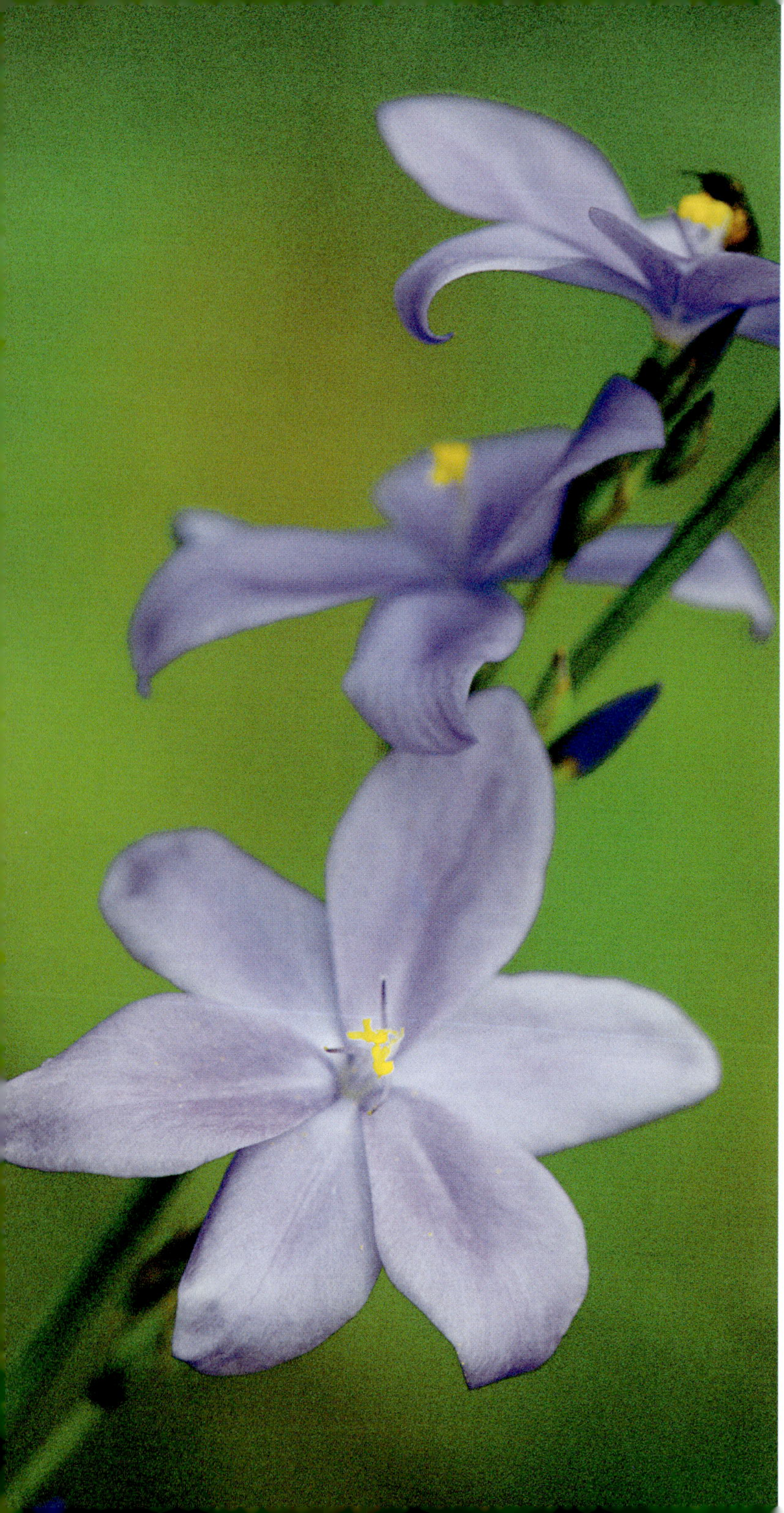

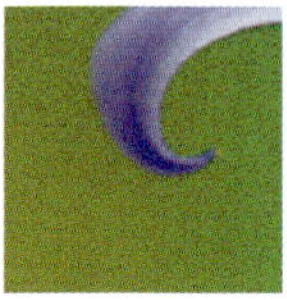

Left:

Morning Iris,

Orthrosanthus

laxus.

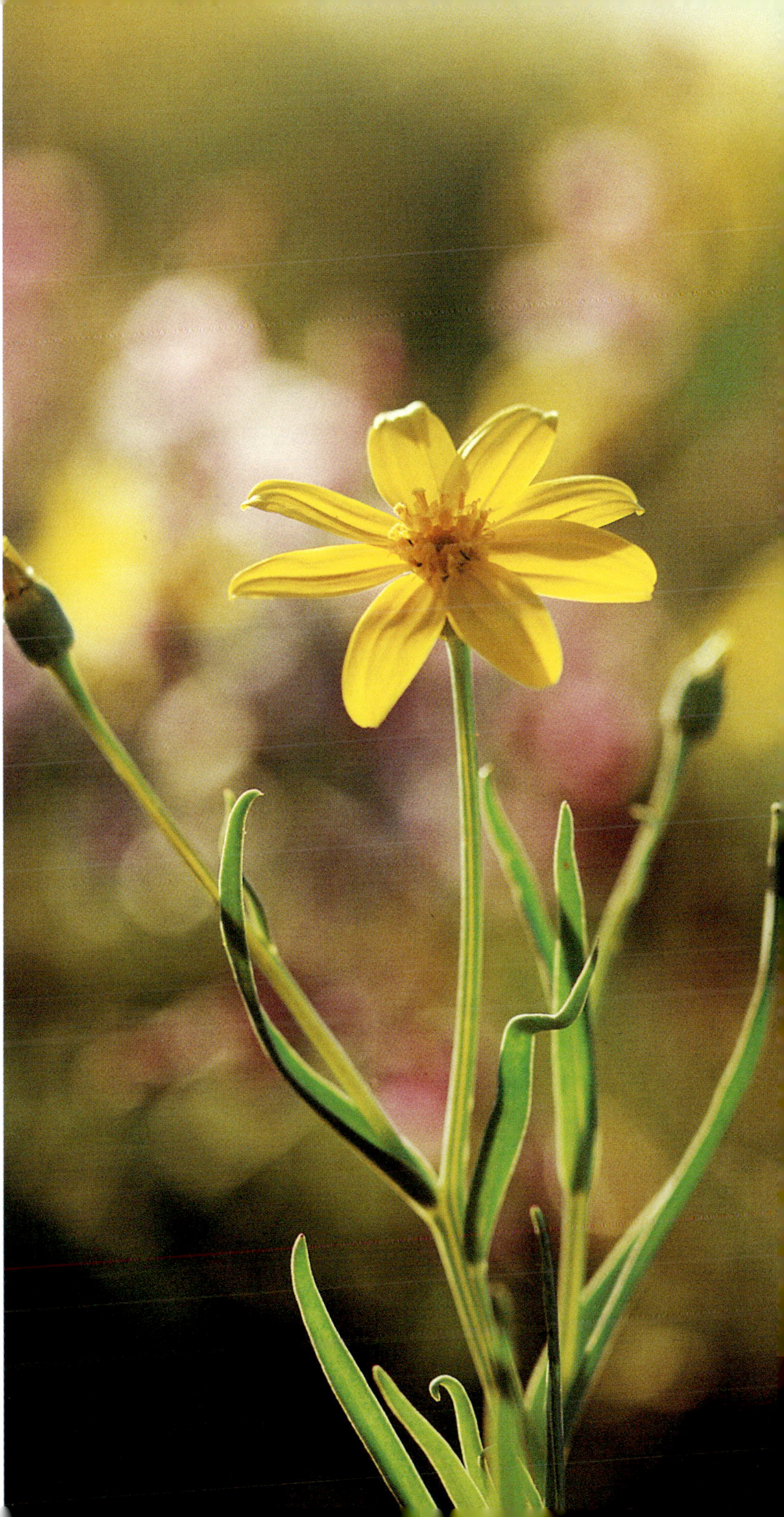

Right:

Yellow Top,

Senecio gregorii.

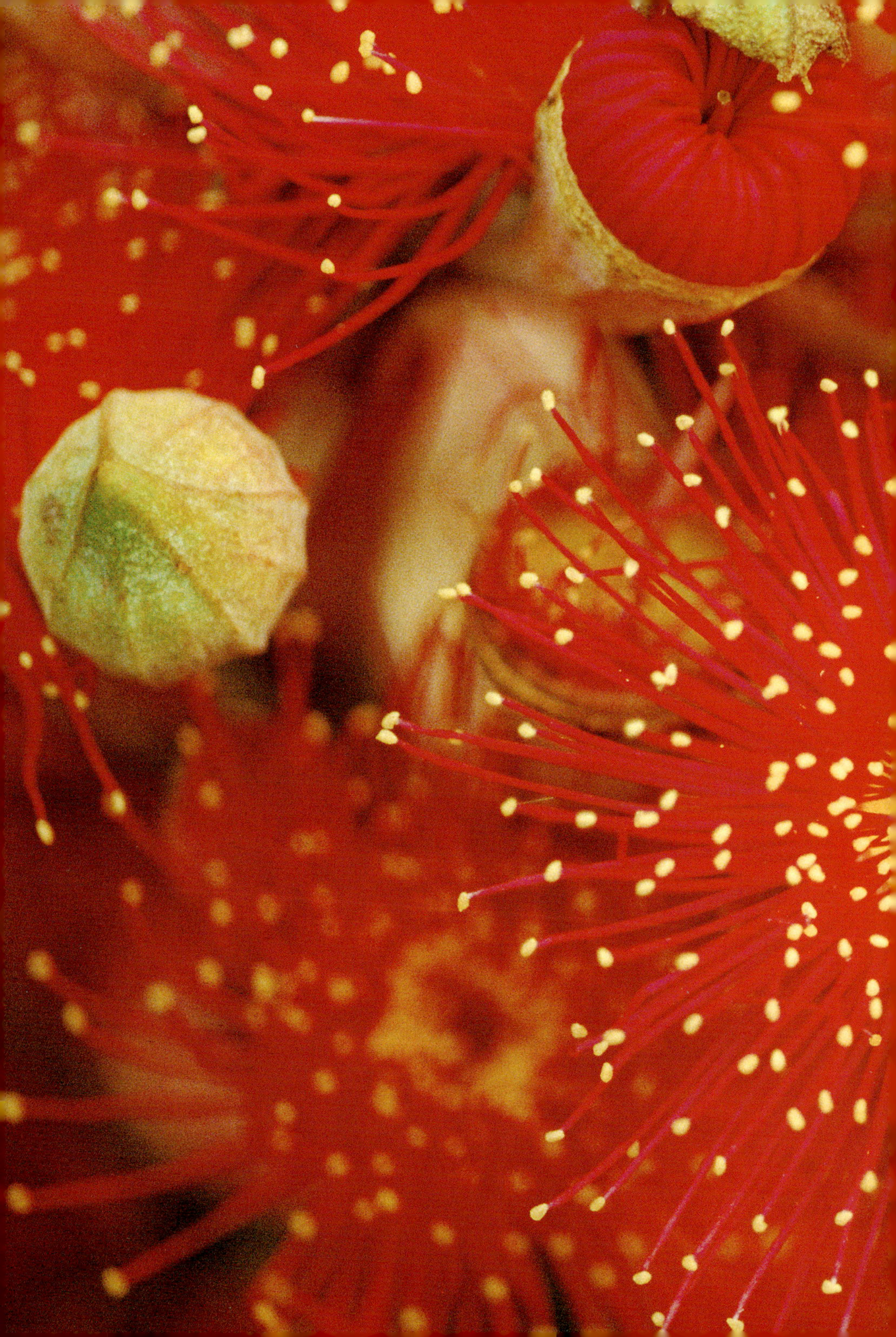

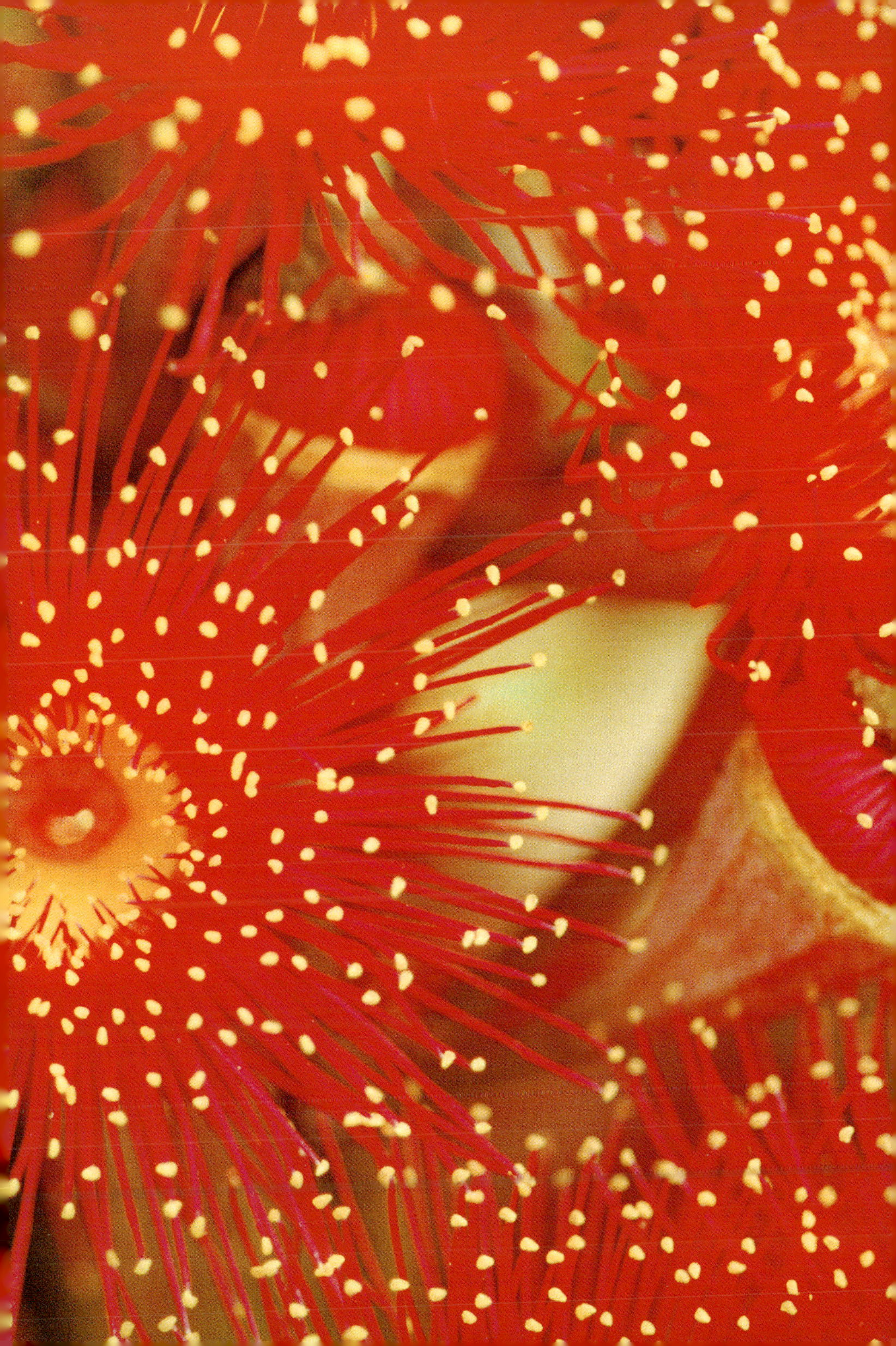

INSPIRATION

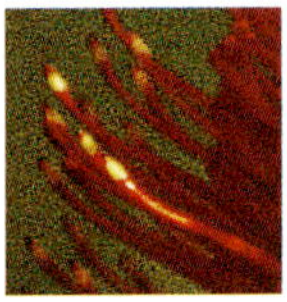

Australia is home to an amazing number and variety of flowering plants, ranging from the showy blossoms of towering gum trees to the hidden beauty of tiny ground orchids. Their colours and shapes delight the eye and defy the imagination.

Pages 24–25: **Swamp Bloodwood, *Eucalyptus ptychocarpa.***

Right: **Yellow Cowslip Orchid, *Caladenia flava.***

Page 27: **Scarlet Banksia, *Banksia coccinea.***

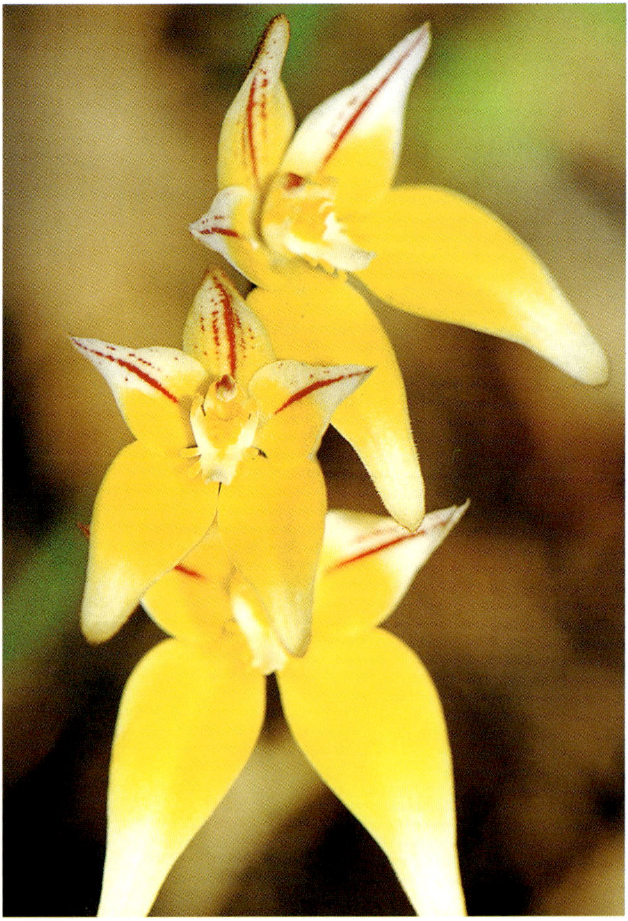

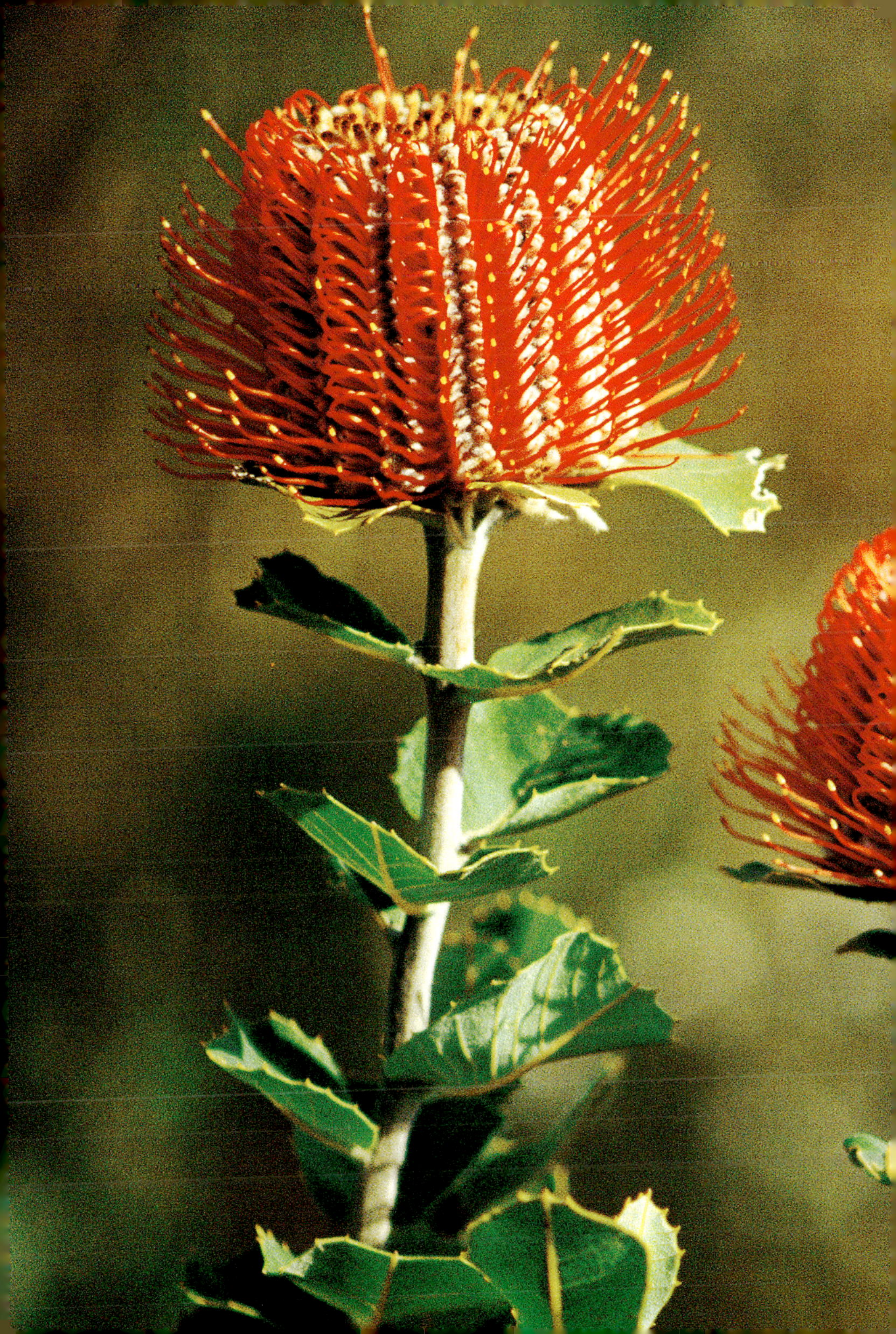

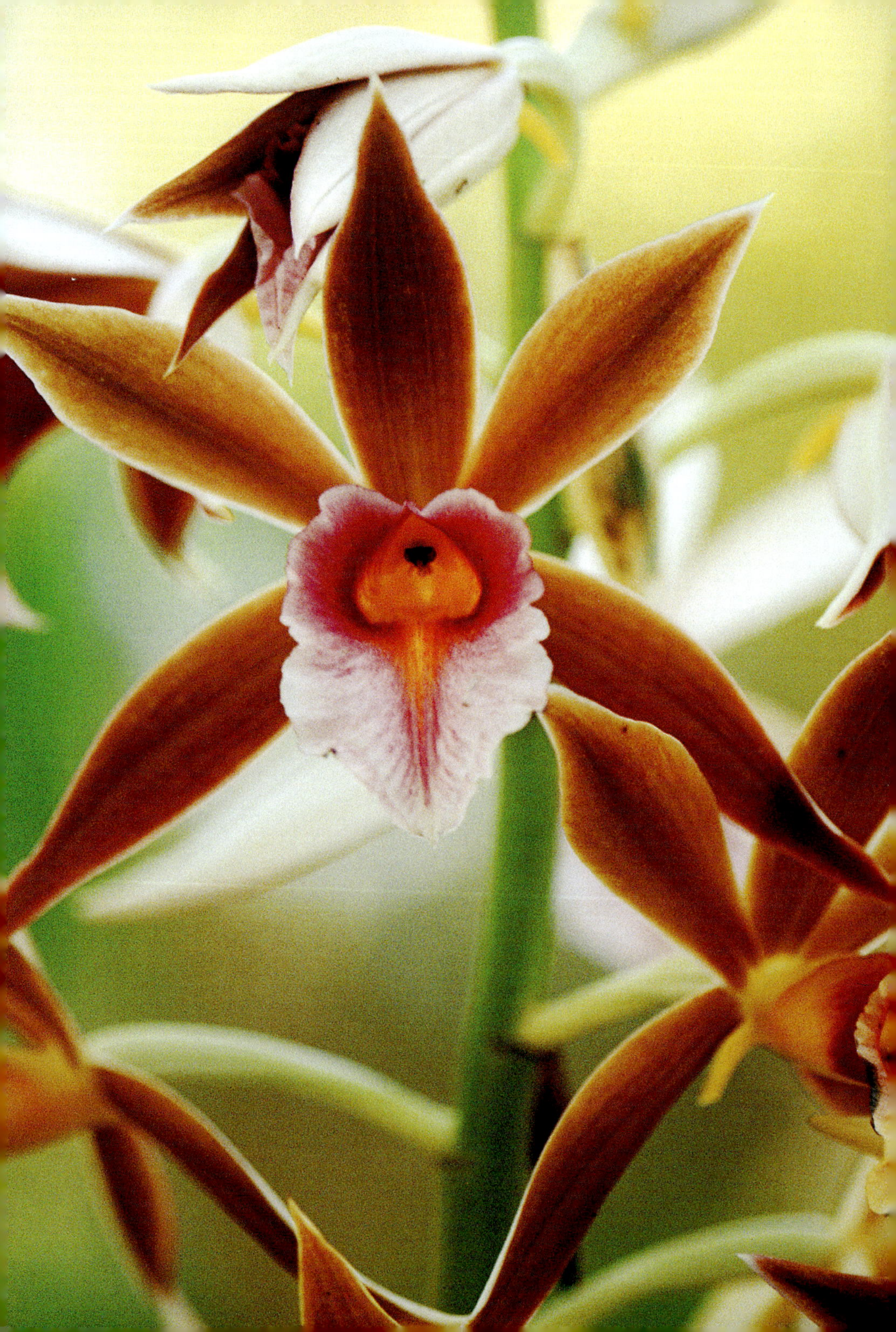

INSPIRATION

Australia's distinctive wildflowers are a continuing source of wonder and inspiration. They are cherished symbols of shared feelings and identity whether it be a simple gesture of love or a proud statement of nationhood.

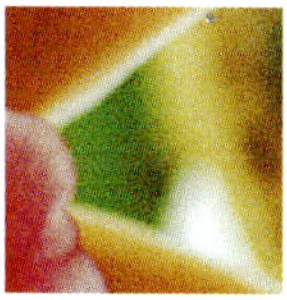

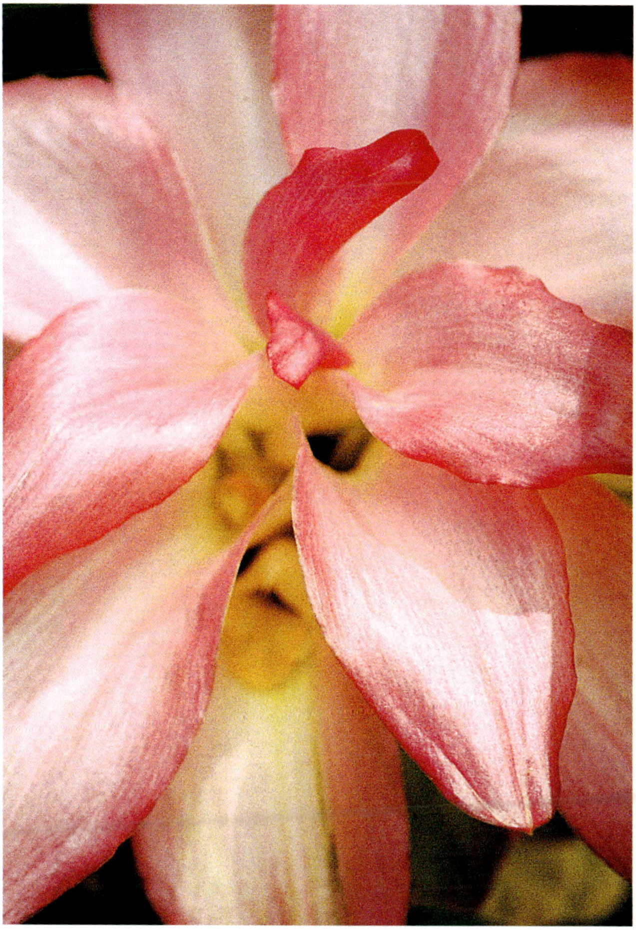

Page 28: **Swamp Orchid, *Phaius tancarvilliae.***

Left: **Cape York Lily, *Curcuma australasica.***

Pages 30–31: **Blue Gum, *Eucalyptus leucoxylon ssp. megalocarpa.***

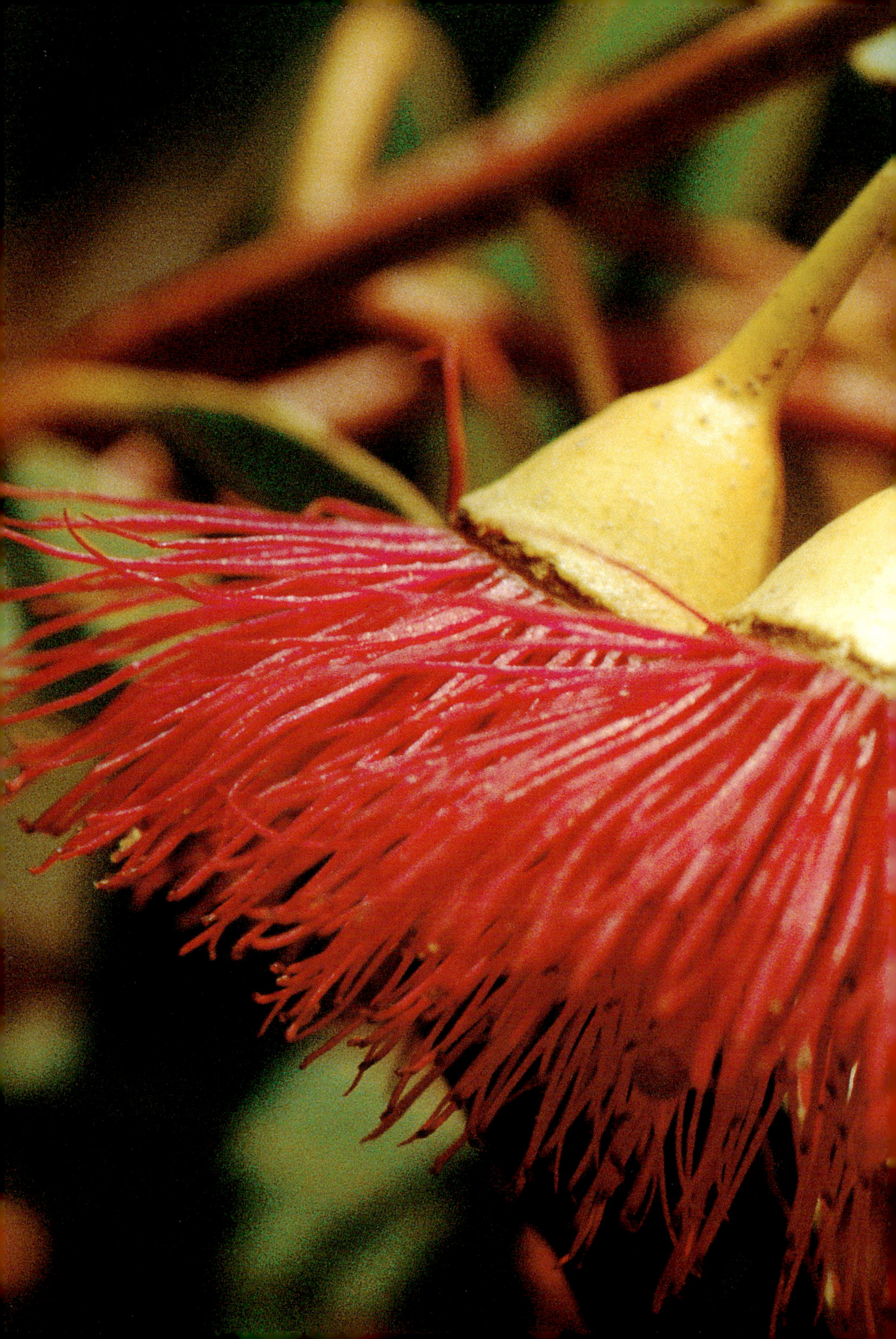

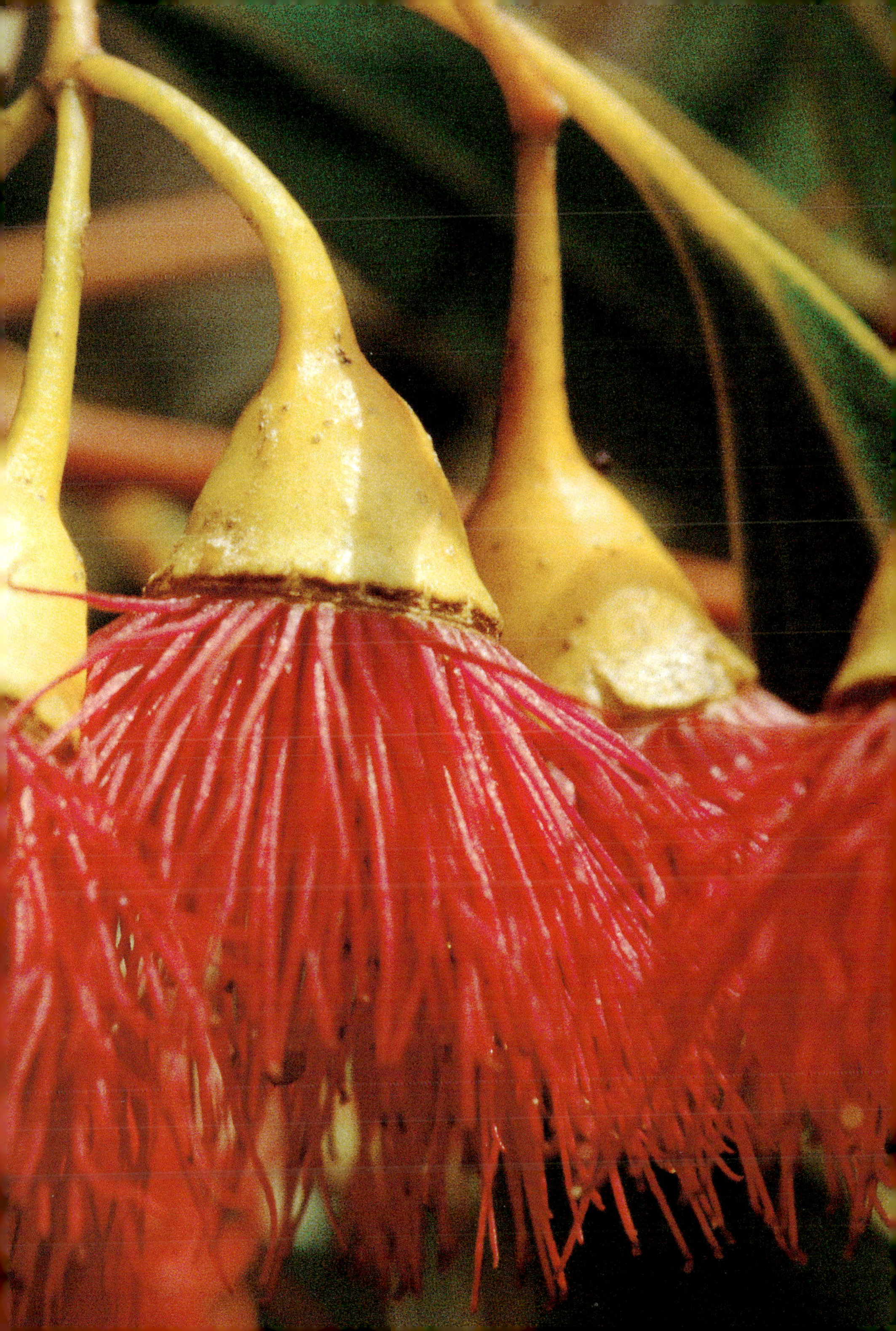

INDEX OF FLOWERS PICTURED

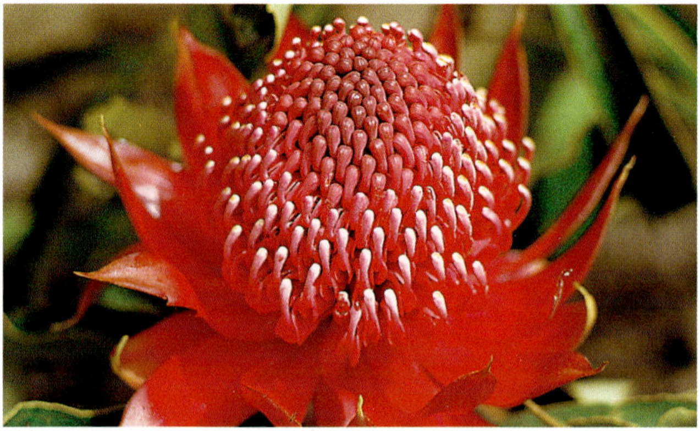

Right: **Waratah, *Telopea speciosissima.***